DATE DUE			
APR -6 '99			
APR 23 '99			
MAY 25 '99			
JUN 21 '99			
AUG 21 00			
OCT 1 0 2002			
JUL 2 8 2003			

J
597.95
MAR   Martin, James

             Chameleons

CHAMELEONS
DRAGONS · IN · THE · TREES

CHAMELEONS
DRAGONS · IN · THE · TREES

by James Martin · photographs by Art Wolfe

CROWN PUBLISHERS, INC. · NEW YORK

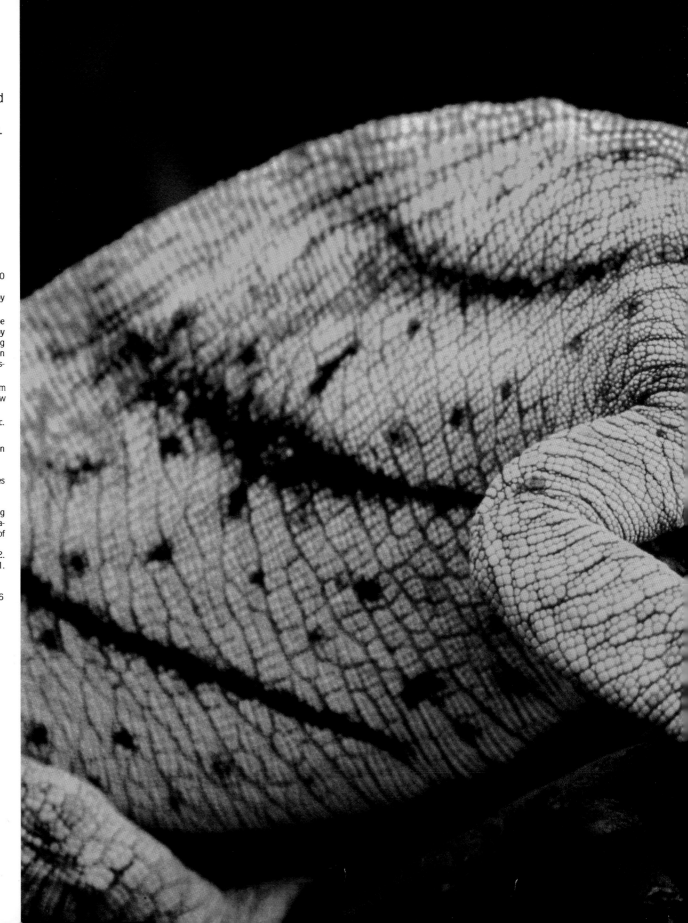

▶Parson's chameleon.
Previous page: Casque-headed
chameleon.
Opening page: Sailfin chameleon.

Published by Crown Publishers, Inc., a Random
House company, 201 East 50th Street, New
York, New York 10022

Crown is a trademark of Crown Publishers, Inc.

Manufactured in Hong Kong

Library of Congress Cataloging-in-Publication
Data
Martin, James
   Chameleons: dragons in the trees/James
Martin; photographs by Art Wolfe.
   p.   cm.
   Summary: Text and photographs introducing
the behavior, African habitat, physical adapta-
tions, endangered status, and other aspects of
several species of chameleon.
   1. Chameleons—Juvenile literature. 2.
Chameleons—Africa—Juvenile literature. [1.
Chameleons.] I. Wolfe, Art, ill.
II. Title.
QL666.L23M36   1991   91-8736
597.95—dc20
ISBN 0-517-58388-7 (trade)
ISBN 0-517-58389-5 (lib. bdg.)
10 9 8 7 6 5 4

Special thanks to Ron and
Marilyn Tremper and the
folks at the San Diego Zoo's
reptile house

Everywhere in Africa
the chameleons watch.
Perched on branches
or standing motionless
on the ground,
their eyes swivel,
looking for danger or food.

◆

Chameleons are reptiles. They live only in Africa and in parts of Asia and Europe. Their skin changes pattern and color. Some grow horns on the end of their noses or above their eyes. On others the back of the head rises like a helmet.

▲ Male Jackson's chameleons have three horns on their heads. Female Jackson's chameleons have one or sometimes none (see photograph on page 8).

▶ Calyptratus chameleon.

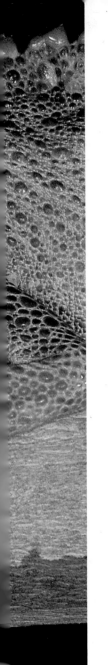

Rows of scales called "crests" decorate their chins and backs, making them look like miniature dragons strutting in the trees. Tails coil like octopus tentacles. Tongues shoot out to snatch insects and other food.

◄ Female Jackson's chameleon.

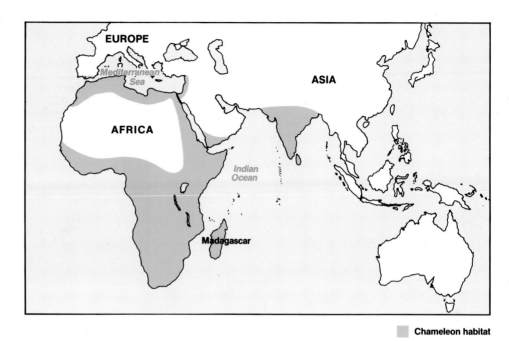

Chameleon habitat

To survive, chameleons must hide. They are too slow to chase the insects they eat or to run away from their enemies, so they must blend in with their surroundings. Unseen and unheard, chameleons live throughout Africa, from the dry sands of the desert to the dripping rain forest. Snow falls on chameleons living high on Africa's tallest mountain, Kilimanjaro. Some of the strangest chameleons inhabit the island of Madagascar, home to many odd and wonderful animals. Rare species are also scattered along the coasts of the Mediterranean Sea and the Indian Ocean. The largest chameleon grows to almost three feet in length; the smallest measures only an inch.

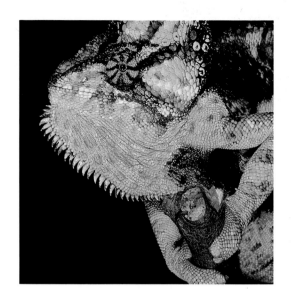 

Some chameleons live under the leaves on the forest floor, but most spend their lives in trees and bushes. The tree-dwelling, or "arboreal," chameleons have V-shaped, smooth-soled feet that can wrap around branches. Their toes are fused together—three on one side of the V and two on the other—to increase the strength of their grip. Their tail acts like a fifth arm, sticking out straight for balance or clutching branches when the climbing gets tricky.

Ground-dwelling chameleons, on the other hand, usually have a short tail that can't hold anything. They are called stump-tailed chameleons. The soles of their V-shaped feet are covered with tiny spiny scales which provide good traction.

▲A calyptratus chameleon grips a branch (*left*). A chameleon's toes are fused together—three on one side of the foot, two on the other (*right*).

▶This casque-headed chameleon is using its tail to help it climb.

◀From above, this casque-headed chameleon is almost invisible against a tree trunk. From the side, its shape stands out clearly.

▶Closeup of the skin of a Meller's chameleon.

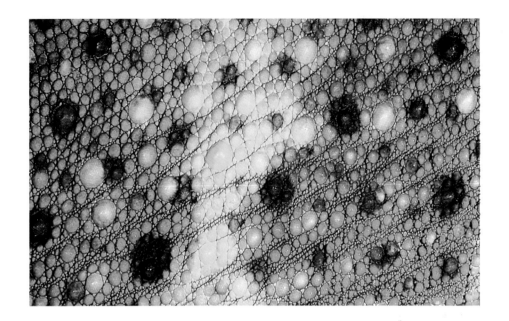

How does such a strange animal stay hidden?

Because their bodies are thin and flat, chameleons resemble the leaves of the bushes and trees they inhabit. But chameleons don't just look like leaves, they also act like them. Instead of marching forward, they hesitate, rocking back and forth like leaves in the breeze. Usually their colors match their surroundings: leaf green, branch brown, and shadow gray.

Chameleons can change color in just a few seconds. Their skin has several layers of special color cells. Each layer controls one color. To change, they expand cells of one color while shrinking others.

Chameleons don't change color in order to hide. They change color in order to communicate with other chameleons. A chameleon's usual color helps it stay hidden. When it meets another chameleon, it changes to a color that is easier to see and that also sends a message to the other chameleon. For example, one combination of colors means "Stay away! This is my bush!" Another means "You win. I'm leaving."

▶ This male pardalis chameleon responds to a threat (his own reflection in a mirror) by covering much of his body with bright yellow instead of his usual green.

▼ A reddened face on the same chameleon signals his readiness to mate. The female's black stripes indicate that she is not willing.

▶ An Oustalet's chameleon puffs out its throat to make itself look larger.

◀ This Senegal chameleon changes from smooth green to black spots and triangles and fills its lungs with air to make itself look larger.

Patterns change as well as colors. The Senegal chameleon shifts from a smooth, uniform green to black and gray, with its sides displaying triangles and polka dots. And the male Jackson's chameleon adds gray diamonds to its usual green.

Chameleons also communicate by pantomime. They have lungs that extend through much of their bodies, enabling them to puff themselves up. They turn sideways, thrusting out their throats and standing tall. Their tails curl in tight spirals. Some species have flaps that they raise above their heads and wiggle. These movements are intended to impress other chameleons and to frighten predators—snakes, birds, and other lizards—by making the chameleon look larger than it really is.

Chameleons react to heat and cold by changing color too. Like all reptiles, they are cold-blooded. Unless they can increase their body temperature by absorbing heat from the sun, they stay the same temperature as the air around them. Without warmth, they can't hunt, move, or digest their food. In the morning they squeeze their sides together and puff out their chins, flattening their bodies to create more surface area. Dark colors absorb heat better, so the side of the chameleon facing the sun becomes almost black, while the other side remains its usual color.

One eye of this calyptratus chameleon looks at the camera. The other eye looks in a completely different direction (*left*). A chameleon's eye is protected by a layer of skin (*right*).

Chameleons have a poor sense of smell and are almost deaf. To compensate, they have marvelous vision. They notice any movement amid the leaves. They even track airplanes flying above them, suspicious that they could be hungry birds. And unlike most reptiles, they see in color.

Chameleons are able to look in two directions at once. They move each eye independently—that is, they can look in one direction with one eye and in a completely different direction with the other eye. Imagine looking in front and in back at the same time without getting confused!

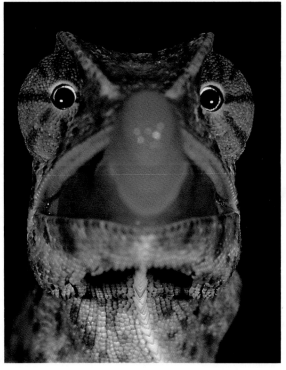

A Senegal chameleon keeps watch (*left*). When it spots an insect, it focuses on the target with both eyes and raises its tongue out of its mouth (*right*).

If you were to chase a chameleon, it would watch you with one eye while looking ahead with the other to see where it was going. Because a chameleon can see in all directions without turning its head, it can remain motionless while looking out for predators and prey alike.

When it's time to eat, chameleons look at their prey with both eyes, which makes them look cross-eyed. To judge distance, both eyes focus on the target at the same time. Then the chameleon quickly hurls out its tongue. If the tongue shoots too far or too short, the chameleon goes hungry.

▲Parson's chameleon.

A chameleon's tongue is its most amazing feature. In
the blink of an eye it can extend farther than the
length of the chameleon's head and body combined.
Depending on the size of the chameleon, the tongue
can pluck a fly from the air or a mouse from the
ground. Without it, this slow, plodding lizard would
starve. Almost anything can run faster than a chameleon.

A Parson's chameleon focuses on its target (*left*), shoots out its tongue (*center*), and swallows an insect (*right*).

After spotting a likely meal, the chameleon brings its tongue to the front of its mouth. A special tongue bone enables the chameleon to raise its tongue out of its mouth and point it at its prey. This bone is tapered at the end like an elongated dunce cap. The tongue is made of circular muscles that fit over the bone like stacked doughnuts. When the "doughnuts" squeeze, the tongue slides to the end of the bone and beyond in a fraction of a second.

▲Jackson's chameleon.

If the tongue hits its target, it sticks. The tip is
rough and covered with a gummy saliva from which
insects and other prey can't escape—although snails,
earthworms, and other slimy things slip off it.
Regardless of whether the chameleon hits or misses,
muscles at the base of the tongue quickly snap the
tongue back into the mouth like a rubber band. But
even when it captures a snack, the chameleon will
start hunting again right away. Wild chameleons are
always hungry.

◀▶ Baby pardalis chameleons.

Most types of chameleons lay eggs. Before laying her eggs, the mother digs a nest in the ground. She digs in the daytime, climbing back to her perch at night to sleep. Chameleons do not move or hunt at night—in fact, they go to sleep as soon as darkness falls.

When the hole is deep enough, the mother lays up to fifty eggs. Chameleons have many babies, because most will be eaten by predators before they grow up. After laying her eggs, the mother covers the nest and hurries back to the heights, never to return. Months later the eggs hatch and the babies dig their way to the surface.

Some species give birth to live young in the trees. The baby chameleon is encased in a thin film that sticks to the branch. After a few moments it struggles free. If the baby falls, it climbs unhurt up the nearest tree to safety.

Whether they are born live or hatched from eggs, baby chameleons are equipped to live on their own from birth. They start hunting with their first steps, their amazing eyes scanning for food. Skinny tongues dart accurately on the first try, and soon a tasty insect becomes the first meal.

▼ Senegal chameleon.

Young chameleons are dull gray or brown. These colors match branches and bark. After growing, they turn the color of leaves. But even when young, they change color if an adult crosses their path.

When alarmed, they puff up as big as they can to frighten the threat, just the way the adults do. If an enemy approaches too closely, the little lizards deliberately fall to the ground. Often the enemy won't follow. At night when they sleep, any movement of their branch causes them to automatically let go and fall to safety.

When frightened, baby chameleons change color and pattern (*left*) and puff themselves up (*right*).

▶A baby Jackson's chameleon, shedding its skin.

Young chameleons pop out of their skins as they grow. The outer layer of skin stops stretching, turns dull, and flakes off, leaving new, brighter skin in its place. Like other lizards, chameleons never stop growing, but they grow fastest, and shed most often, in the first year of life.

▼Baby pardalis chameleon.

▶ Casque-headed chameleon.

No one knows how long chameleons live in the wild. Jackson's chameleons have lived almost ten years in captivity, but they may live longer when free.

Like many animals, chameleons face a shrinking habitat. The forests are disappearing in Africa as people cut trees to make room for fields to feed an exploding population. Almost all the forests of Madagascar are gone, forcing many species into pockets of parkland, where they struggle to survive. Local people collect them and sell them to traders, who ship them to pet stores. If too many are collected, species die out.

Most pet chameleons die within weeks. Many suffer from disease and are weak after the long trip from Africa without food, water, or space to move. They require certain amounts of sun and temperature variation to stay healthy. In fact, many people believe they need to be free in order to live. They die when faced with life in a terrarium.

▼ Pardalis chameleon.

◀ Pardalis chameleon.

To prevent extinctions, scientists around the world are trying to raise chameleons in captivity. But chameleons are very sensitive. If conditions are not just right, they will not breed. So far only a few types have been born in captivity.

Recognizing the threat to their wild animals, many of the countries where chameleons live are protecting the land and the animals that live there. Some ban the export of chameleons for sale as pets. If these efforts succeed, these harmless dragons will continue to haunt the forests and plains and mountains of Africa. When people visit, they will always be watched by unseen eyes.

Index

About reptiles

Reptiles have lived on earth for more than 300 million years—since before the age of the dinosaurs, and far longer than human beings. They are divided into groups called "orders," the most important of which are tortoises and turtles, crocodiles and alligators, and snakes and lizards.

Chameleons are lizards. Lizards usually have five toes on their feet, eyelids to cover their eyes, and ears visible on their heads. Snakes have none of these things. Like all reptiles, lizards are cold-blooded, which means that their bodies remain the same temperature as the air around them. If they get too cold, they cannot move or hunt and will eventually die.

There are one hundred different species of chameleon. They live in Africa, Madagascar, parts of Asia, and on the Mediterranean coasts of some European countries. The slim green lizards that are sometimes called chameleons and that are sold at carnivals in the United States are not true chameleons. Rather, they are members of the anole family of lizards, which live in the Americas.

About the authors

James Martin is a freelance writer and photographer living in Seattle. He has visited Africa, Madagascar, and Borneo, and has studied the world's largest lizard, the Komodo dragon, on Komodo Island in Indonesia. His work has appeared in *Smithsonian, Sports Illustrated, Boy's Life*, and other publications. This is his first book for children. Art Wolfe also lives in Seattle. He is one of America's leading nature photographers. He has photographed many books, including studies of owls and bears, and a survey of North American wildlife entitled *The Kingdom*; his work has also been widely published in magazines, journals, and calendars.